50 STATES ACTIVITY BOOK

DK

DK | Penguin Random House

Authors Laura Buller, Jolyon Goddard
Illustrator Jenny Wren c/o Advocate Art Ltd

Project Editor Robin Moul
Project Art Editor Victoria Palastanga
US Senior Editors Shannon Beatty, Lori Hand
Designers Karen Hood, Sadie Thomas, Eleanor Bates, Rachael Hare
Subject Consultant Eric Peterson
Senior DTP Designer Tarun Sharma
Producer Basia Ossowska
Jacket designer Charlotte Milner
Jacket Coordinator Issy Walsh
Picture Researcher Sakshi Saluja
Managing Editor Penny Smith
Managing Art Editor Mabel Chan
Creative Director Helen Senior
Publishing Director Sarah Larter

First American Edition, 2021
Published in the United States by DK Publishing
1450 Broadway, Suite 801, New York, NY 10018

Copyright © 2021 Dorling Kindersley Limited
DK, a Division of Penguin Random House LLC
20 21 22 23 10 9 8 7 6 5 4 3 2 1
001-323609-May/2021

All rights reserved.
Without limiting the rights under the copyright reserved above, no part of this publication may be reproduced, stored in or introduced into a retrieval system, or transmitted, in any form, or by any means (electronic, mechanical, photocopying, recording, or otherwise), without the prior written permission of the copyright owner.
Published in Great Britain by Dorling Kindersley Limited

A catalog record for this book is available from the Library of Congress.
ISBN 978-0-7440-3800-2

DK books are available at special discounts when purchased in bulk for sales promotions, premiums, fund-raising, or educational use. For details, contact: DK Publishing Special Markets, 1450 Broadway, Suite 801, New York, NY 10018
SpecialSales@dk.com

Printed and bound in China

For the curious
www.dk.com

MIX
Paper from responsible sources
FSC www.fsc.org FSC™ C018179

This book was made with Forest Stewardship Council ™ certified paper - one small step in DK's commitment to a sustainable future.
For more information go to www.dk.com/our-green-pledge

DK would like to thank: Jacqueline Hornberger for proofreading and Eric Peterson for factchecking.

Picture Credits
The publisher would like to thank the following for their kind permission to reproduce their photographs:
(Key: a-above; b-below/bottom; c-center; f-far; l-left; r-right; t-top)

3 **Dreamstime.com:** Chorthip (br); Maksym Kapliuk (tl); Rck953 (tr); Sonya Etchison (clb). 4 **123RF.com:** arcady31 (bc). **Dreamstime.com:** Maksym Kapliuk (ca). 5 **Dreamstime.com:** Brian Kushner (cr). 6 **Dreamstime.com:** Chicco7 (br); Dannyphoto80 (c); Pongpon Rinthaisong (crb); Jia He (fcrb); Kwiktor (cb); Leigh Anne Meeks (crb/Lifeguard Stand); **Fashionstock.com** (cb/skier); Viavaltours (fcrb/water ride). 7 **Dreamstime.com:** Bgsmith / Brandon Smith (cr); Nerthuz (tc); Martin Schneiter (bl). 8 **Dorling Kindersley:** Roskilde Viking Ships Museum, Denmark (fbl). **Dreamstime.com:** Anthony Baggett (clb); Maxim Grebeshkov (tc); Dannyphoto80 (bl). **Getty Images:** Maarten Wouters (tr). 9 **Dreamstime.com:** Maxim Grebeshkov (cla). 10 **123RF.com:** akulamatiau (clb); Svetlana Yefimkina (bl, cra/maple); Anton Starikov (crb). **Dreamstime.com:** Marc Bruxelle (tl, tr, bl/red maple); Maxim Grebeshkov (tc); Svetlana Larina / Blair_witch (cra/Butterfly); Anna Derzhina (cb); Pamela Mcadams (cb/pancake); Nevinates (cb/Blueberries); Igor Zakharevich (br); Serezniy (br/strawberry). 11 **123RF.com:** arcady31 (cla). **Dreamstime.com:** Bodik1992 (c); Maxim Grebeshkov (tr); Yekaterinalimanova (cra). **Getty Images / iStock:** DigitalVision Vectors / Ani_Ka (ca/waves). 12 **Dreamstime.com:** Maxim Grebeshkov (tr). 13 **Dreamstime.com:** Cynoclub (cb/mouse); Maxim Grebeshkov (ca); Dannyphoto80 (b/background); William Wise (clb); Jnjhuz (bl); Iakov Filimonov (crb). **Fotolia:** Vadim Yerofeyev (bc). 14 **123RF.com:** aivolie (tr); mediagram (cr). **Dreamstime.com:** Betelgejze (c/background); Maxim Grebeshkov (ca/flag); Vldmr / Vladimir Zadvinskii (t/leaves x4); Denys Kurylow (cla); Evgenii Kazantsev (br). 15 **123RF.com:** mediagram (cr). **Dreamstime.com:** Hypnotype / Evgeny Skidanov (clb); Luciano Mortula (tr); Liron Peer (b/signs x14). 16 **Dreamstime.com:** Dzmitryshashko (cra, tl); Maxim Grebeshkov (tr); Pavel Naumov (crb); Jay O'brien (cl). **Getty Images / iStock:** StartStock (cra/tractor). 17 **123RF.com:** Anna Zakharchenko (c/x9). **Dreamstime.com:** Marc Bruxelle (bc); Maxim Grebeshkov (tr). 18 **123RF.com:** utima (bc). **Dreamstime.com:** Maxim Grebeshkov (crb); Linda Harms (tr). 19 **123RF.com:** Anna Zakharchenko (fcl, bc). **Alamy Stock Photo:** IanDagnall Computing (tl). **Dreamstime.com:** Jon Bilous (cra); Maxim Grebeshkov (cl); Iconisa (cl/bridge, cr). 20 **123RF.com:** skellos (background). **Dreamstime.com:** Maxim Grebeshkov (tr). 21 **123RF.com:** solomonjee (crb); Visions of America LLC (clb). **Dreamstime.com**: Avmedved (fclb); Maxim Grebeshkov (ca); Tristana / Kseniya Abramova (tc); Maryart / Maria Itina (tl); Lunamarina (cb). **Getty Images / iStock:** DigitalVision Vectors / Ani_Ka (cla/waves). 22 **Dreamstime.com:** Maxim Grebeshkov (ca); Photographieundmehr (tl/oak leaf x2); Zentilia (tr). **Getty Images / iStock:** angkritth (cb, br). 23 **Dreamstime.com:** Roman Egorov (ca/background); Maxim Grebeshkov (cla); Ekaterina Mikhailova (ca). 24 **123RF.com:** James Cumming (ca). **Dreamstime.com:** Steve Byland (cla); Maxim Grebeshkov (cra); Sgoodwin4813 (tr); Petar Kremenarov (cl); Eric Isselée (cl/horse); Svetlana Foote (clb); Michael Truchon (cb). 25 **Dorling Kindersley:** Alan Murphy (cl/kingfisher). **Dreamstime.com:** Musat Christian (clb); Maxim Grebeshkov (cra); Isselee (cla, cl). 26 **Dreamstime.com:** Maxim Grebeshkov (cra); Anton Ignatenco (tl); Hugoht (cr). 27 **Dorling Kindersley:** Astro Info Service Ltd / Dave Shayler (cb). **Dreamstime.com:** Maxim Grebeshkov (crb); Saddako123 / Svetlana Foote (br). 28 **123RF.com:** dahlia (cb/background); weenvector (bl, bc). **Alamy Stock Photo:** D. Hurst (cra). **Dreamstime.com:** Sonya Etchison (cr); Maxim Grebeshkov (tr); Daniel Logan (cb). 29 **123RF.com:** Saichol Modepradit (b/background). **Dreamstime.com:** Svetlana Foote (cl); Nylakatara2013 (ca); Isselee (clb). **Rex by Shutterstock:** AP / Rogelio V Solis (tr). 30 **123RF.com:** Martin Damen (tl). **Dreamstime.com:** Acanonguy / Tony Northrup (bl); Maxim Grebeshkov (br); Zrfphoto (tr). 31 **123RF.com:** Leysan Shayakbirova (fcra). **Alamy Stock Photo:** Kyoko Uchida (bl). **Dreamstime.com:** Furtseff (cr); Maxim Grebeshkov (fcr); Imagecom (cra); Boris Medvedev (fcrb); Yifang Zhao (br, crb). 32 **Dreamstime.com:** Michael Flippo (bl); Maxim Grebeshkov (tr). 33 **Dreamstime.com:** Maxim Grebeshkov (tr); Sneekerp (cra). 34 **Dreamstime.com:** Maxim Grebeshkov (cb, fcrb, crb); Showvector (cra); Chris Turner (cr); Laralova (br). 35 **Dreamstime.com:** Maxim Grebeshkov (cl); Jktu21 (ca/skyline). 36 **Dreamstime.com:** Etiennevoss (c); Maxim Grebeshkov (tr); Mchudo (crb); Gatito33 (ca). 37 **Dreamstime.com:** Maxim Grebeshkov (cra). **Getty Images / iStock:** ballycroy (tr). 38 123RF.com: newgena (crb). **Dorling Kindersley:** Natural History Museum, London (cra/jaw). **Dreamstime.com:** Maxim Grebeshkov (cra). 39 **Dreamstime.com:** Maxim Grebeshkov (tr). **Getty Images / iStock:** angkritth (bl); Quirky Mundo (cb). 40 **Dreamstime.com:** John Anderson (cr); Maxim Grebeshkov (ca); Jeka84 (tl); Claudio Momberto (c); Irina Kozhemyakina (clb); Musat Christian (crb). **Getty Images / iStock:** DigitalVision Vectors / filo (ca/corns). 41 **123RF.com:** alhovik (clb); Martin Damen (cb); scanrail (c). **Alamy Stock Photo:** Art Directors & Trip / Donna Ikenberry (cra). **Dreamstime.com:** Maxim Grebeshkov (cl); Hanna Tsiarleyeva (cla); Marion Wear (ca); Ekaterina Mikhailova (cb/tractor). 42 **Dreamstime.com:** Maxim Grebeshkov (ca); Hanna Tsiarleyeva (br). 43 **Alamy Stock Photo:** Everett Collection Inc / Courtesy: CSU Archives (clb). **Dreamstime.com:** Maxim Grebeshkov (crb); Irochka (tl). **Photolibrary:** FoodCollection (cra). 44 **123RF.com:** alhovik (bc); Eric Isselee / isselee (tr). **Dreamstime.com:** Jose Carvalho (c); Maxim Grebeshkov (crb). 45 **Dreamstime.com:** Maxim Grebeshkov (tc); Rico Leffanta (tr); Vertyr (ca); Timothy Grover (fclb); Marazem (crb); Kravtzov (clb); Pamela Mcadams (fcrb). 46 **Dreamstime.com:** Aks980 (cla); Maxim Grebeshkov (cra); VetraKori (cl, c); Narupon Nimpaiboon (cl/cactus flower). **Getty Images / iStock:** Quirky Mundo (b). 47 **Dreamstime.com:** Maxim Grebeshkov (tr); Hhurzhi (ca, cra); SaveJungle (c). 48 **123RF.com:** Fotoplanner (cla, cr). **Dreamstime.com:** Maxim Grebeshkov (ca); Anna Kucherova / Photomaru (tr). 49 **123RF.com:** Fotoplanner (b); mediagram (b/trees). **Dreamstime.com:** Dragoneye (br); Maxim Grebeshkov (clb). 50 **123RF.com:** Iegor Zhukovetskyi (cla, cl). **Alamy Stock Photo:** All Canada Photos / Darwin Wiggett (cb); Svetlana Foote (cb/Bear). **Dreamstime.com:** Maxim Grebeshkov (cra); Denys Kryvyi (t/Background, b). **Getty Images / iStock:** DNY59 (bl, br). 51 **Alamy Stock Photo:** Feng Yu (c). **Dorling Kindersley:** Natural History Museum, London (fbr, br). **Dreamstime.com:** Maxim Grebeshkov (bc); Denys Kryvyi (cr). 52 **123RF.com:** Iegor Zhukovetskyi (ca, cra, crb). **Dreamstime.com:** Maxim Grebeshkov (cr); Edwin Verin (tl). **Maze Generator:** (c). 53 **123RF.com:** Anna Zakharchenko (cla, cra). **Alamy Stock Photo:** Agefotostock / George Ostertag (bc). **Dreamstime.com:** Maxim Grebeshkov (crb); Welcomia (c); Manel Vinuesa (cb/Virginia); Superjoseph (cb/Hoover Dam); Renzzo (br). **Getty Images / iStock:** dzubanovska. **Getty Images:** Sylvain Sonnet (cb). 54-55 **Dreamstime.com:** Vladimir Kolesnikov. 54 **Alamy Stock Photo:** All Canada Photos / Darwin Wiggett (cb); Julie Quarry (cr); Mark Conlin (crb/x3). **Dreamstime.com:** Maxim Grebeshkov (cra); Yuval Helfman (cb/Otter); Hotshotsworldwide (bc). **Getty Images / iStock:** Michael Zeigler (c). 55 **123RF.com:** Mariusz Blach (tc); Anna Zakharchenko (ca, c). 56 **Dorling Kindersley:** Jerry Young (clb). **Dreamstime.com:** Maxim Grebeshkov (br). 57 **123RF.com:** Visarute Angkatavanich (clb/phone). **Alamy Stock Photo:** NASA Archive (cb). **Dreamstime.com:** Axstokes (fclb); Maxim Grebeshkov (c); Marekp (cb/USB); Fredweiss (tl); Natalia Bystrova (crb); Pnwnature (bc). 58 **123RF.com:** Vladimir Ovchinnikov (cr). **Dreamstime.com:** Robert Adrian Hillman / (Microsoft th) (Microsoft Corporation Edition) (bl, crb); Maxim Grebeshkov (tl); suriya silsaksom khunaspix@yahoo.co.th (cl). **Getty Images / iStock:** zackwool (fcl). 59 **Dreamstime.com:** Chorthip (cl, tr). **Getty Images / iStock:** marrio31 (cb); tiler84 (cra); Westend61 (c). 60-61 **Dreamstime.com:** Iakov Filimonov / Jackf; Rawin Thienwichitr (t). 61 **123RF.com:** Russ McElroy / russ9358 (cra); Ricard Vaque (www.vaque.com) (br); Ihor Obraztsov (tl, tc, tl/Plane); youngID (tc/Cycle). **Dreamstime.com:** Maxim Grebeshkov (clb); Jeanninebryan (cla). **Getty Images / iStock:** mantaphoto (c). **Getty Images:** TCYuen (cr). 62 **123RF.com:** Anna Zakharchenko (cra). **Dreamstime.com:** Cynoclub (c/mouse); William Wise (c/Deer); Iakov Filimonov (c/Wolf); Dannyphoto80 (c/Background, c/forest); Jnjhuz (c/Beaver). **Fotolia:** Vadim Yerofeyev (c). 63 **Dorling Kindersley:** Alan Murphy (cla/Kingfisher). **Dreamstime.com:** Musat Christian (cla/beaver); Svetlana Foote (tc/armadillo); Isselee (cla/otter, tc/spoonbill, cla). 64 **123RF.com:** Visarute Angkatavanich (cr). **Alamy Stock Photo:** NASA Archive (cr/Analog Machine). **Dreamstime.com:** Axstokes (c); Marekp (cr/USB); Hhurzhi (bl); SaveJungle (bl/Maze Background). **Maze Generator:** (cb). 66 **Dreamstime.com:** Maxim Grebeshkov (x49); Maksym Kapliuk (tc). **Rex by Shutterstock:** AP / Rogelio V Solis (c). 67 **123RF.com:** Ewastudio (br); Dullatum Hanrud (bl); skellos (b/Background). **Alamy Stock Photo:** Joe McDonald / Steve Bloom Images (clb). **Dreamstime.com:** Chee-onn Leong / Coleong (ca); Jorge Salcedo / Jorgeantonio (cra); Luayana (c). 70 **123RF.com:** John McAllister (bc/Fawn). **Dreamstime.com:** Lukas Blazek / Lukyslukys (cb); Rck953 (c); VetraKori (clb); Marion Wear (bc); Geoffrey Kuchera (crb/Kit); Melinda Fawver (br). **Getty Images / iStock:** DigitalVision Vectors / filo (bl); VladGans (crb). 71 **Alamy Stock Photo:** Robertharding / Michael Nolan (cra). **Dreamstime.com:** Boldurevaol (tl); Ivonne Wierink (tr); Jay Pierstorff (cla); Gale Verhague (ca); Sumikophoto (ca/Javelina); Spvvkr (clb); Mirko Vitali / Viewapart (cb/Hollywood); Petthomas (crb); Shane Myers (bl); Isselee (cb/Tang). **Fotolia:** Alexander Edmonds (cb). **Getty Images / iStock:** miroslav_1 (fclb)

Cover images: *Front:* **123RF.com:** María Elena Garcia Huertas clb, Jakobradlgruber tl, Sean Pavone br; **Dreamstime.com:** Maksym Kapliuk crb; **Getty Images / iStock:** Stellalevi cra; *Back:* **123RF.com:** Sean Pavone bl

All other images © Dorling Kindersley
For further information see: www.dkimages.com

CONTENTS

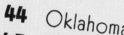

Alaska is actually bigger than Texas.

☐ Alaska

Make your own US flag using this one as a guide. Use stickers for the 50 state stars.

FUN FACT
The number of stars on the flag has changed over the years as states were added. The stripes represent the 13 colonies.

☐ Wisconsin

☐ Washington

☐ Montana

☐ North Dakota

☐ Minnesota

☐ Oregon

☐ Idaho

☐ South Dakota

☐ Wyoming

☐ Nevada

☐ Utah

☐ Colorado

☐ Nebraska

☐ Iowa

☐ California

☐ Kansas

☐ Missouri

☐ Arizona

☐ New Mexico

☐ Oklahoma

☐ Arkansas

☐ Texas

☐ Hawaii is 2,400 miles away from California to the southwest.

N
W   E
S

☐ Louisiana

THE 50 STATES

Welcome to the third-biggest country in the world. All kinds of people and wildlife call America home, and this diversity has made each of the 50 states unique. Let's get to know more about the 50 states—the places you've already been, and the states you get to discover for the first time.

☐ Michigan

Lake Superior

The Great Lakes

Lake Huron

Lake Michigan

☐ Vermont

☐ Maine

Lake Erie

☐ New York

☐ Pennsylvania

☐ inois   ☐ Indiana   ☐ Ohio

☐ West Virginia   ☐ Virginia

☐ Kentucky

☐ Tennessee

☐ North Carolina

☐ South Carolina

☐ Alabama   ☐ Georgia

☐ Mississippi

☐ Florida

CHECK OFF THE STATES WHEN YOU FINISH THE ACTIVITY PAGE.

☐ New Hampshire
☐ Massachusetts
☐ Rhode Island
☐ Connecticut
☐ New Jersey
☐ Delaware
☐ Maryland

REGIONS OF AMERICA

This map shows the six regions that are often used to divide up the states. There are also smaller regions within these larger groups, such as New England in the Northeast, and the Great Lakes in the Midwest.

☐ West   ☐ Southeast   ☐ Midwest

☐ Southwest   ☐ Northeast   ☐ Non-contiguous states

ACROSS THE 50 STATES

The United States is so large it has all kinds of landscapes to explore—from sandy beaches to majestic mountains, scorching deserts to mighty rivers. History, culture, and wildlife also vary from state to state, making America an incredible country to explore.

MY FAVORITE STATE

Do you have a favorite state? Is it where you live now, or where you'd love to be? Find it in the book, and fill in the key facts here.

State name

_____

Capital

_____

Abbreviation

_____

Statehood

_____

Nickname

_____

State flower

_____

State animal

_____

MY TRAVEL MAP

Draw the outline of your favorite state—you can find the shape of each state in the map on pages 4 and 5. Now use your map to plot all the places that are important to you. Have you visited any cities in this state? Is there a famous landmark you'd like to see? Read about your favorite state in this book if you need some ideas.

MY PERFECT VACATION

There are so many things to see and do across America. Whether you like sun or snow, cities or forests, you'll find a perfect vacation spot right here in the United States. Try this quiz to help you find your ultimate vacation destination.

Skiing in Vermont

Sightseeing in New York

Exploring Denali National Park

Camping at the Great Lakes

Relaxing in Hawaii

Going to an Orlando resort

Visiting San Diego Zoo

DO YOU LIKE BIG CITIES? — YES / NO

DO YOU LIKE SPORTS? — YES / NO

DO YOU PREFER WINTER OR SUMMER? — WINTER / SUMMER

DO YOU LIKE CAMPING? — YES / NO

DO YOU LIKE GOING TO THE BEACH? — YES / NO

DO YOU LIKE THEME PARKS? — YES / NO

GREAT STATE SOUVENIRS

When you're traveling, it's fun to bring home a souvenir to remind you of your trip. Most states are famous for a certain symbol—like a food or an animal—so these symbols make great souvenirs. If you had $15, what would you like to buy from this list? Can you figure out which states these items represent?

STATUE OF LIBERTY FIGURINE $6

MAPLE SYRUP $2.50

SEA OTTER CUDDLY TOY $8

TOY ROCKET $5

POPCORN KEYRING $3.50

COWBOY HAT $10

COUNTRY COLLAGE

America is a huge country, so you can expect all kinds of different scenery and wildlife as you travel across the 50 states. Some states are famous for one type of landscape, while others have a variety. What kinds of scenery is your home famous for?

Q&A
What is the nickname of your favorite state?

Spot 11 differences in these American landscapes.

MAINE

STICK THE STATE FLAG HERE →

With thousands of miles of coastline and more forests than any other state, Maine is a real natural beauty. Its forests are home to a huge variety of animals, as is the water along the Atlantic Coast, where seals, whales, and lobsters can be found.

FUN FACT
Could you eat a buttered bug? Maine's coastal waters are home to lots of lobsters, which are actually close relatives of the insect family. Mainers sometimes call them bugs.

OH, BUOY!

Fishers in Maine catch lobsters in underwater traps. Each trap has a floating buoy with a colored pattern that's unique to each person. Draw a line to match up each fishers with the correct buoy.

My buoy is red, white, and blue.

My buoy has two red bands.

My buoy is mostly white.

My buoy is mostly red.

THE VIKINGS

Maine is one of the nine states in the Northeast region. In the 1700s, many Europeans arrived in this region to start a new life in America. But an ancient penny discovered in Maine is a clue that the Vikings may have been the first Europeans to arrive, some 1,000 years ago. Use "runes," the Viking alphabet, to work out these Viking themed words.

ᚨᚠᛁᛏᛖ _____

ᛒᛖᚾᛏᛗ _____

ᚠᚨᛖᚱᛁᛤᚠ _____

ᛗᚢᚱᚠᛖᛗ _____

RUNIC ALPHABET:

ᚠᛒᛚᚨᛗᛖᛘᚷᚷᚻᛁ ᛣᛤᚱᚨᛏᛶ ᚠᛖᚷᚠᛦᛐᛏᚢᚹᛁᛘᛗᛉ
A B C D E F G H I J K L M N O P Q R S T U V W X Y Z

NEW HAMPSHIRE

From the snow-capped peaks of White Mountain National Park down to the sandy Atlantic shores, New Hampshire is a wild and wonderful state. It's beautiful all year round, but it may be at its best when the leaves turn red in the fall.

STICK THE STATE FLAG HERE

FUN FACT
The first free public library in the US was the Dublin Juvenile Library. It opened in Dublin, New Hampshire, in 1822.

FALL LEAVES

New England is made up of six states in the Northeast region. It's famous for its beautiful scenery, especially in the fall when the leaves turn red and gold. Take a look at this fall scene and see if you can spot all the things on these lists.

COUNT UP:
How many people are taking pictures?

_____

How many dogs are there?

_____

FIND AND CIRCLE:

VERMONT

STICK THE STATE FLAG HERE

Before it joined the United States, Vermont had its own money, stamps, and president. Vermont is now popular for winter fun, with many great ski resorts. Three-fourths of the land is covered in forest, and the state is famous for its maple syrup made from local tree sap.

FUN FACT

A legendary monster with silver scales and the head of a seahorse is said to lurk in the depths of Lake Champlain. Nicknamed Champ, the monster is protected by Vermont law, just in case it is real.

STATE SYMBOLS

Across the country, people like to choose symbols to represent the culture, history, and natural beauty of their state. Can you find these state symbols for Vermont in the grid? They're scattered up, down, across, and diagonally.

H	W	R	Y	N	S	E	T	M
M	O	E	R	I	H	S	C	O
A	I	N	X	N	O	A	P	N
R	R	G	L	E	A	P	P	B	A
T	N	D	K	Y	L	P	E	R
L	Z	I	G	C	B	L	G	C
E	Y	T	A	H	I	E	A	H
R	E	D	C	L	O	V	E	R

State beverage: **MILK**   State fruit: **APPLE**

State flower: **RED CLOVER**   State insect: **HONEYBEE**

State butterfly: **MONARCH**

MAPLE SYRUP

Vermont's delicious maple syrup goes great with breakfast foods. If you had $10.00 to spend, what would you want to order for breakfast?

HOW MUCH MONEY DO YOU HAVE LEFT?

GLASS OF MILK $1.50

SILVER DOLLAR PANCAKES $3.50

ORANGE JUICE $2.50

BLUEBERRY TOPPING $2.00

MINI BOTTLE OF SYRUP $3.00

WAFFLES $5.50

PANCAKES WITH SYRUP $4.50

STRAWBERRY TOPPING $2.50

MASSACHUSETTS

Rich in history, Massachusetts is sometimes called the birthplace of the United States. The Pilgrims landed at Plymouth Rock, the revolution against British rule started here, and Massachusetts also helped lead the United States into its age of industry.

STICK
THE STATE
FLAG HERE

PLYMOUTH
ROCK

START
HERE

THE
MAYFLOWER

FUN FACT

There's a lake in Webster, Massachusetts with a long Algonquian name:

MAYFLOWER MAZE

In 1620, passengers boarded a ship called the *Mayflower* in Plymouth, England. They set sail for America, and eventually settled as the Plymouth Colony in Massachusetts. Can you help the ship cross the Atlantic Ocean to reach America?

LAKE CHARGOGGAGOGGMANCHAUGGAGOGGCHAUBUNAGUNGAMAUGG

Because it's such a long name, people also call it Webster Lake for short.

FAMOUS SIGHTS

Massachusetts has so much to see and do, from historic sights and beautiful scenery to exciting cities and seaside towns. Can you unscramble the names of these famous spots in Massachusetts?

apeC doC

_____

A perfect summer vacation desitation

eedFrom raiTl

_____

A famous walkway through Revolutionary War sites in Boston

darvHar sityiverUn

_____

The country's oldest university

RHODE ISLAND

Rhode Island may be a tiny state, but it's packed with history, culture, and lots of natural beauty. Having more than 400 miles of coastline means that everyone can hit the beach in less than half an hour.

↑
STICK
THE STATE
FLAG HERE

ON THE COAST

Rhode Islands needs a lot of lighthouses to help warn ships about the nearby coastline. Colorful stripes, triangles, or other shapes help them stand out in the daytime. These patterns are called "daymarks." Make up your own daymarks for this lighthouse.

FUN FACT

While Rhode Island is larger than some entire countries, it is the smallest state in the US. You could fit more than 3,000 Rhode Islands into the whole United States!

THE 13 COLONIES

British colonists originally settled in 13 colonies along the East Coast. Here, the states representing the 13 colonies have been jumbled up.

CAN YOU NAME THE STATES FROM THEIR OUTLINES?

(If you need help, look at the map on pages 4 and 5.)

- [ ] New Hampshire
- [ ] Massachusetts
- [ ] Rhode Island
- [ ] Connecticut
- [ ] New York
- [ ] New Jersey
- [ ] Pennsylvania
- [ ] Delaware
- [ ] Maryland
- [ ] Virginia
- [ ] North Carolina
- [ ] South Carolina
- [ ] Georgia

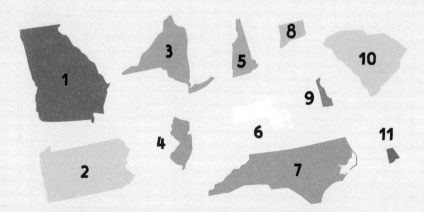

Nickname: The Ocean State   State flower: Violet   State bird: Rhode Island Red chicken

CONNECTICUT

Connecticut's cities are home to some of the most famous colleges in America. The land is made up of steep hills, volcanic valleys, sparkling rivers, and thick forests. In fact, some 60 percent of the state is made up of forest. These woods are home to bobcats, bears, and white-tailed deer.

FUN FACT
In 1909, Connecticut became the first state to introduce a speed limit for automobiles. It was set at just 12 miles per hour.

ANIMAL TRACKS
Some 40 different species of mammal live in Connecticut's woodlands. Wherever they go, they make their mark with tracks on the ground. Draw a line to connect the animal to its tracks on the signpost. One has been done for you as an example.

↑
STICK
THE STATE
FLAG HERE

Q&A
True or false:
Connecticut was one
of the 13 colonies?

Mouse

Deer

MATCH THE TRACKS:

Beaver

Wolf

Bear

Raccoon

NEW YORK

New York City dazzles with its many famous landmarks, while the rest of New York state is full of natural beauty. There are waterways, lakes, and wetlands, and the land is covered in mountains, forests, and pretty countrysides that are fun to explore in any season.

FUN FACT
Niagara Falls is a group of waterfalls on the New York-Canada border. There are two smaller falls on the New York side, and a giant one on the Canadian side.

STICK THE STATE FLAG HERE

GREAT OUTDOORS

New York has a variety of natural scenery to explore, with something for every season. There are beaches on Long Island, lots of lakes for water sports, and great hiking and camping north of New York City. It gets really cold in winter, so you can also ski and ice-skate.

Find these outdoors-themed words in the grid?

SKATING
ISLAND
BEACHES
LAKES
CAMPING
SNOW
HIKING
KAYAK

P	C	A	M	P	I	N	G	E	R
O	O	I	N	U	W	F	S	V	H
S	E	S	O	L	O	N	L	I	I
S	K	A	T	I	N	G	E	N	K
I	N	A	T	S	K	N	K	S	I
G	N	O	Y	L	O	S	L	I	N
I	J	R	W	A	F	I	A	E	G
L	K	S	O	N	K	R	K	I	L
O	I	P	A	D	A	M	E	A	W
J	B	E	A	C	H	E	S	R	

Q&A
True or false: New York is the only state that borders the Great Lakes. Check the map on pages 4 and 5 if you need a hint.

NEW YORK, NEW YORK

New York City is home to millions of proud New Yorkers—it's the most populous city in the United States. It's also full of tourists who come to visit famous landmarks like the Statue of Liberty and Empire State Building. Look at this busy city scene and see if you can spot the items in the list.

CAN YOU SPOT...

HOW MANY FLAGS CAN YOU SEE? _____

 1
 2
 3
 4
 5
 6
 7
 8
 9
 10

THOUSAND ISLANDS

New York is famous for its lakes and rivers, like the Finger Lakes and Thousand Islands region. Some say this is the namesake for Thousand Island dressing. Despite the region's name, there are actually more than 1,000 islands.

Use American Sign Language to find out how many islands there really are in this region.

_____ _____ _____ _____

PENNSYLVANIA

STICK IN THE STATE FLAG

Pennsylvania's multicultural cities have given the US some of its tastiest treats. They are also full of interesting sights, from the Liberty Bell—a symbol of American freedom—to the traditional spring forecast made by a famous animal.

FUN FACT

Philadelphia Zoo opened in 1874. It was the very first zoo in the United States.

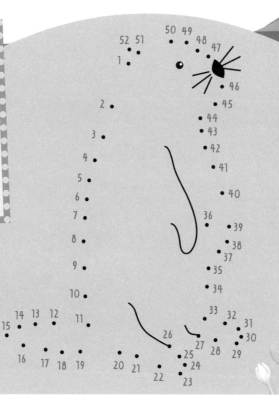

SPRING FORECAST

Which animal is said to predict the start of spring in Pennsylvania? Complete the dot-to-dot and fill in the name below to figure it out.

G _ o _ _ d h _ g

Q&A

Which famous symbol of American freedom can be found in the state of Pennsylvania?

FOOD-OKU

Pennsylvania introduced these four foods to the United States. Some were brought by foreign settlers, while others were invented here. Fill in this grid with these four foods. Each row and column can only contain one of each food.

WHOOPIE PIE

CHEESESTEAK

SHOOFLY PIE

PRETZEL

NEW JERSEY

STICK IN THE STATE FLAG

New Jersey is one of the smallest states, but its population is the 11th highest of all the 50 states. During the hot summers, people beat the heat by heading to the state's sandy beaches.

FUN FACT
The board game Monopoly is based on Atlantic City in New Jersey.

BEACH MAZE

New Jersey's coastline is known as the Jersey Shore. It's full of great attractions, including fishing villages and amusement parks. But most people go "down the shore" for its beautiful sandy beaches.

Help Isabel find her way through this sand maze to the ice cream vendor at the end.

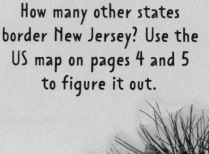

FOREST TREES

New Jersey isn't just about beaches. It also has many forests dotted around the state. Unscramble the names for these trees that grow in the forests here.

kOa

_____

yorHick

_____

pelMa

_____

Q&A
How many other states border New Jersey? Use the US map on pages 4 and 5 to figure it out.

hceeB

_____

neiP

_____

Capital: Dover   Abbreviation: DE   Statehood: 1787; 1st state

DELAWARE

Delaware's hills slope down to swamps and beaches, and all kinds of animals live here. The rich soil in the state is great for farming, and you'll find plenty of top crops in the state. Although Delaware is small, it has a big place in history because it was the first American state.

MAP IT

Delaware is the second smallest state in the country. Can you put these states in the correct order, from smallest (6) to largest (1)? You can use the map on pages 4 and 5 to help you.

DELAWARE _____   ALASKA _____

SOUTH DAKOTA _____   TEXAS _____   NORTH DAKOTA _____   RHODE ISLAND _____

FUN FACT

Delaware is part of the Southeast region, which is made up of 14 states. The Southeast has rich farmlands, and deposits of coal and oil that fuel the economy.

STICK THE STATE FLAG HERE

1   2   3   4   5

SUPER STRAWBERRIES

Delaware's official state fruit is the delicious strawberry. No one knows how this plant got to North America, but Indigenous peoples had been harvesting them since the 1600s. Can you put the life cycle of this sweet fruit in the right order?

MARYLAND

This state is famous for its coastal towns and beaches. It is also home to wonderful national parks, such as the Harriet Tubman Underground Railroad National Historical Park. Tubman, who was born in Maryland, helped lead many slaves to freedom.

HARRIET TUBMAN

CHESAPEAKE BAY BRIDGE

DOODLE NOODLE

Maryland's Chesapeake Bay Bridge is an amazing 4.3 miles long. Because the bridge is tall, narrow, and the weather is often windy, some people think it's one of the scariest trips across water!

HOTEL

Can you design your own bridge across an ocean bay?

STICK THE STATE FLAG HERE

MARINE LIFE

Maryland is home to miles of sandy beaches, and resorts like Ocean City draw huge crowds. The state is famous for its seafood, especially blue crab, but the oceans aren't just for fishing up food. Can you find the names of Maryland's amazing marine life in this word search?

Some words may run backward.

CRAB
DOLPHIN
SEAL
PORPOISE
TURTLE
WHALE
OYSTER
JELLYFISH
SHARK

P	Q	Y	F	F	A	D	L	E	M
O	M	I	O	W	A	O	S	V	H
R	U	E	Y	U	M	L	A	E	S
P	I	M	S	N	I	P	O	L	I
O	B	Y	T	G	R	H	O	O	F
I	E	A	E	E	O	I	W	S	Y
S	H	A	R	K	P	N	H	A	L
E	K	E	O	C	I	H	A	E	L
E	A	P	O	J	E	R	L	A	E
L	E	T	U	R	T	L	E	P	J

WEST VIRGINIA

West Virginia is the only state that is completely inside the Appalachian Mountains. It's packed with beautiful mountains, hills, rivers, gorges, and waterfalls, and all kinds of animals roam these wild lands.

↑
STICK IN
THE STATE
FLAG

WILD WEST VIRGINIA

Here are some animals that live in this state. Place the animal sticker next to the matching clue and fill in its name.

Q&A

Read this page and see if you can figure out why West Virginia is known as "The Mountain State."

FUN FACT

The people of West Virginia must really love music, because in 1963 they chose three official state songs instead of just one. In 2014, they even added a fourth state song: the famous country song "Take Me Home, Country Roads."

They can't really fly, but they can glide.

_____
_____

They can use their claws to climb trees. They are also the state mammal.

_____

Every year, the males grow new antlers.

_____

Their babies are called kittens.

_____

Males are called drakes, and females are called hens.

_____

They sleep in trees at night.

_____

Nickname: The Mountain State   State flower: Rhododendron   State mammal: Black bear

VIRGINIA

Virginia is famous for its history. It was the site of early European settlements, Civil War battlefields, and home to many presidents. It's also a beautiful state, with beaches, mountains, and rich farmlands.

FUN FACT

Have you heard of the "wild" horses that roam Virginia's Assateague Island? They may be descendants of domestic horses that were released on the island in the 17th century.

STICK IN THE STATE FLAG

AMERICAN DOGWOOD

HISTORIC VIRGINIA

In 1610, colonists from England made their first permanent settlement in America at Jamestown. There the settlers met the Indigenous Powhatan people, who were already living in this area. Can you find the words linked to these two groups?

Hint: some words may run backward or diagonally.

CORN
VIRGINIA
JAMESTOWN
POWHATAN
COLONY
SHIP
SETTLER

N	Q	A	A	H	T	T	R	E	S
A	S	I	N	U	W	F	S	V	B
T	E	E	O	L	Y	N	Y	I	A
A	I	P	T	S	N	E	N	R	S
H	M	O	I	T	O	W	O	G	H
W	E	N	B	E	L	S	C	I	I
O	J	Y	U	D	O	E	O	N	P
P	K	S	O	V	C	R	R	I	L
O	I	P	A	R	A	M	N	A	W
J	A	M	E	S	T	O	W	N	S

WASHINGTON, D.C.

The nation's capital is close to Virginia, but it is not actually part of any state. The name "D.C." stands for District of Columbia—it means the capital is in its own district. Can you fill in the names these important D.C. buildings?

The tallest structure in the city.

Celebrates one of Virginia's most famous residents (and presidents!)

Its address—1600 Pennsylvania Avenue—is as famous as its residents.

W _ s h _ n _ t _ _
M _ n u _ e _ t

J _ ff _ _ s _ n   M _ mo _ _ al

_ h _   Wh _ _ e
_ o _ se

KENTUCKY

Kentucky is a state of beautiful countryside scenery. Almost half the state is covered in forests. Its nickname is "The Bluegrass State," but the grass is actually a bluish-green. Many farms dot the grassy plains and hills here, and you'll spot lots of horses galloping in the fields.

FUN FACT

Fort Knox Bullion Depository is one of the world's largest underground gold vaults. The gold bars there are worth more than $200 billion.

Q&A

How many other states border Kentucky? Hint: use the US map on pages 4 and 5 to figure it out.

STICK THE STATE FLAG HERE

CORN MAZES

Corn is a common crop grown on the farms of Kentucky. It can grow to be taller than a person, so some farms plant corn mazes for people to explore. Can you help Noah find his way out of the maze?

MYSTERY ANIMAL

Many wild animals roam Kentucky, but the state is famous for an animal that is raised at special farms here. They also compete in a big race called the Kentucky Derby. Complete the connect-the-dots to find out what animal it is.

TENNESSEE

Tennessee is dotted with rugged mountains soaring above valleys, plains, and farmland. Great Smoky Mountains National Park lies on its eastern border. Tennessee is famous for its music, and artists like Elvis Presley have lived and worked in the music capitals of Bristol, Memphis, and Nashville.

← STICK THE STATE FLAG HERE

FUN FACT
Some of the most amazing landmarks in Tennessee are underground. It's home to the Lost Sea, the largest underground lake in the US.

MUSIC FESTIVAL

Music is an important part of Tennessee's culture and history. A lot of musicians have come to this state to develop the sounds of country music, rock and roll, and the blues.

HOW MANY?
This music festival is full of people who have come to enjoy new music. Write down how many of these items you can spot.

GUITARS ____

ICE CREAMS ____

SAXOPHONES ____

FIND AND CIRCLE

Someone who dropped their ice cream

A person in a red-and-white-striped dress

A baby in a cowboy hat

Someone in white boots

NORTH CAROLINA

From peaks more than a mile high to sandy beaches, North Carolina is a state packed with natural beauty. More than half the state is covered in forests, home to black bears, raccoons, coyotes, and many birds.

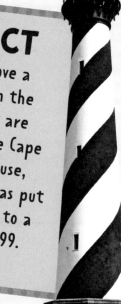

FUN FACT
How do you move a lighthouse when the sands around it are washing away? The Cape Hatteras lighthouse, tallest in the US, was put on rails and rolled to a new location in 1999.

← STICK THE STATE FLAG HERE

NATURE SPOT

Practice being a nature spotter with this tic-tac-toe game. This is a game to play in pairs. Every time you spot a new animal from the grid, the first person to call out the name can mark it off. The first person to complete three in a row is the winner.

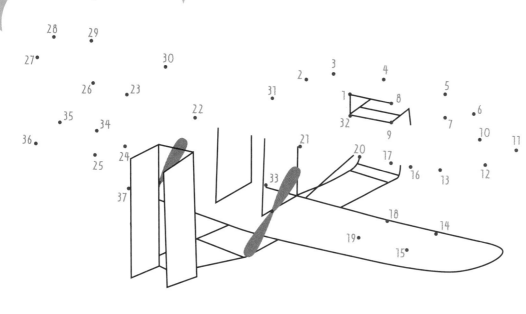

INCREDIBLE INVENTION

The Wright brothers, Orville and Wilbur, experimented with an amazing contraption. They needed to find a place with strong winds and open space to test it. They came to Kitty Hawk, North Carolina, and history was made. Connect the dots to find out what they built.

SOUTH CAROLINA

The sandy beaches of South Carolina are popular vacation spots. You can also find sand on top of South Carolina's mountains, because this region used to be part of the Atlantic Ocean. Deep forests cover much of the state, and lots of amazing wildlife can be found around South Carolina's wetlands, swamps, and rivers.

STICK IN THE STATE FLAG

DINNERTIME

Here are some of South Carolina's wetland critters. Follow the lines and place in the correct stickers to find out each animal's favorite food.

FUN FACTS

People once used wood from the palmetto tree–the spiky one on the state flag–to build forts. The spongy wood helped soften the blow of cannonballs during the Revolutionary War.

DAY AT THE BEACH

South Carolina's coast has some great beaches, as well as whole islands to explore. These friends are spending the day at Myrtle Beach, and want to buy some ice cream. How much will each one cost?

1 SCOOP = $1

2 SCOOPS = $2

SPRINKLES = $0.50

CHOCOLATE SAUCE = $0.75

2 scoops with sprinkles, please.

AVA

2 scoops, sauce, and sprinkles, please.

ELIJAH

1 scoop with sauce, please.

WILLIAM

GEORGIA

Georgia is known as the Peach State because it has been producing this tasty fruit for hundreds of years. Georgia is also famous for the Blue Ridge Mountains, the country's largest aquarium, and the world's busiest airport.

STICK
THE STATE
FLAG HERE

GEORGIA FACTS

Can you unscramble these Georgia-themed words? You can find them all on this page.

talanAt ——————   muriAqua ——————

torpAir ——————   eaPches ——————

Trearsue ——————   Mounstain ——————

FLY AWAY

More than 107 million passengers roll their bags through Atlanta's Hartsfield-Jackson Airport in a typical year. It's the busiest airport in the world, and Georgia's largest employer. Follow the wiggly lines and help this family get through the busy airport to their plane.

FUN FACT

Georgia's islands are legendary for stories of buried treasure. Blackbeard Island was named for Edward Teach, a pirate who raided countless ships in the early 18th century. His loot has never been found.

Nickname: The Peach State   State flower: Cherokee rose   State marine mammal: Right whale

FLORIDA

Florida is almost completely surrounded by water, from the Gulf of Mexico around to the Atlantic Ocean. Its sandy beaches, sunny weather, amazing scenery, and theme parks make it popular with tourists.

FUN FACT

The flattest state is not out in the Great Plains. It's Florida! Back in prehistoric times, the whole state was underwater.

BLAST OFF!

For more than 70 years, rockets have soared into the skies from Florida's Space Coast. Can you figure out the name of the rocket that was used for the first moon landing? Look at the numbers below, then use the cypher on the right to work out the letters.

| 19 | 1 | 20 | 21 | 18 | 14 | 22 |

_ _ _ _ _ _ _

A=1	B=2	C=3	D=4	E=5
F=6	G=7	H=8	I=9	J=10
K=11	L=12	M=13	N=14	
O=15	P=16	Q=17	R=18	
S=19	T=20	U=21	V=22	
W=23	X=24	Y=25	Z=26	

GATORS AND CROCS

The Everglades is the only place in the world where alligators and crocodiles live together. The two species may look similar, but there are a lot of differences. Draw a line from these facts to the correct animal.

ROUND SNOUT

LONG, POINTY SNOUT

USUALLY DARKER IN COLOR

USUALLY LIGHTER IN COLOR

HAS A LONGER BODY

HAS A SHORTER BODY

ALLIGATOR

CROCODILE

STICK THE STATE FLAG HERE

Q&A
True or false: both crocodiles and alligators live in the Everglades.

ALABAMA

Alabama stretches from the Appalachian Highlands in the north to the Gulf Coast wetlands in the south. It's the birthplace of author and political activist, Helen Keller. She overcame great adversity to become the first blind-deaf person to earn a college degree.

UP, UP, AND AWAY!

Each May, a hot-air balloon festival is held in the city of Decatur. The festival began in 1978, and now attracts thousands of visitors who come to watch the balloon race. Try designing your own balloon for the festival.

STICK THE STATE FLAG HERE

FUN FACT

The Saturn V rocket, which helped Apollo astronauts get to the moon, was designed at the Marshall Space Flight Center, in Huntsville, Alabama.

Q&A

In which year was the first hot-air balloon festival held in Decatur, Alabama?

STATE SUDOKU

Can you fill in this sudoku grid with four of Alabama's state symbols? Every row and column can only contain one of each symbol—no doubles allowed.

State mammal:
BLACK BEAR

State bird:
YELLOWHAMMER

State nut:
PECAN

State berry:
BLACKBERRY

MISSISSIPPI

Mississippi is well known for its music and literature, but it's even more famous for its rivers. The state is named for the Mississippi River, which forms most of the state's western border. It also has many other rivers and lakes, creating lots of swampy areas.

STICK THE STATE FLAG HERE

FUN FACT

The Mississippi Petrified Forest is the remains of an ancient forest that turned into rock over millions of years.

← PETRIFIED WOOD

BEASTS OF THE BAYOU

Bayous are swampy wetlands. They are full of interesting wildlife. Follow the wiggly lines to match each of these animals with their favorite food.

ARMADILLO

ALLIGATOR

SPOONBILL

BOBCAT

SMALL CRAB

MUSKRAT

ANT

CATFISH

MISSISSIPPI MUD PIE MATH

Have you tried Mississippi mud pie? People all over the world love this chocolatey dessert. Can you figure out what fraction of each pie is left over?

/2   /4   /3

O n _ - h _ _ f   T h _ e _ - f _ u r _ h s   T w _ - _ h i _ d s

ARKANSAS

Arkansas is a landlocked state with its capital city, Little Rock, right at its heart. The state has many natural spots to exlore, like Hot Springs National Park, and its cities have lots of great attractions.

APPLE BLOSSOM

CALL OF THE WILD

Every year in Stuttgart, Arkansas, there's a contest to see who can copy the call of a certain animal. You can even take a class to improve your animal call. Finish this connect-the-dots to find out which animal they try to mimic in this competition.

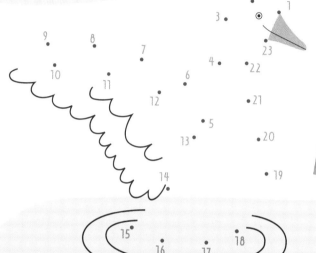

FUN FACT

The temperature of the naturally heated water at Hot Springs National Park is a scalding 143°F.

H	X	K	C	O	R	E	L	T	T	I	L
O	V	M	H	K	L	B	I	O	E	R	O
T	O	B	A	C	J	E	E	N	X	N	S
S	Z	P	R	O	G	E	R	S	A	R	P
P	X	V	R	W	O	B	E	T	R	I	R
R	O	R	I	G	S	E	E	N	K	S	I
I	R	D	S	L	T	A	M	L	A	X	N
N	B	X	O	B	E	N	T	O	N	F	G
G	C	O	N	W	A	Y	C	K	A	E	D
S	T	N	G	S	I	P	R	S	E	U	A
R	O	H	Z	C	Y	A	Y	E	V	G	L
F	A	Y	E	T	T	E	V	I	L	L	E

Word list:
ALMA
BEEBE
BENTON
CABOT
CONWAY
FAYETTEVILLE
HARRISON
HOT SPRINGS
LITTLE ROCK
ROGERS
SPRINGDALE
TEXARKANA

URBAN ARKANSAS

The state capital, Little Rock, is also Arkansas's biggest city. But there are lots of other cities and fun sightseeing spots in the state. Can you find these Arkansas cities hidden in the word search? Hint: some may run backward.

STICK THE STATE FLAG HERE

LOUISIANA

Louisiana is known for lots of different things, from the hot and humid climate to its mouthwatering Creole cuisine. It's especially famous for the vibrant city of New Orleans.

FUN FACT
The Mardi Gras street parades and festivities attract millions of visitors to New Orleans each year.

DELICIOUS DESSERTS

Louisiana is famous for its food. Follow your nose and find your way through the windy city streets to a bakery selling yummy, deep-fried beignets.

BEIGNETS

ALL THAT JAZZ!

Louisiana is famous for jazz, a type of music created by African Americans in the city of New Orleans. Can you unscramble the names of these intruments, and draw a line to the correct picture?

STICK THE STATE FLAG HERE

petTrum
T _ _ m _ e _

umDrs
_ r _ _ s

onaiP
_ i _ n _

Saphoxone
_ _ x _ p h _ _ e

netariCl
C _ a _ _ n e _

ombTrone
T _ _ m b _ _ e

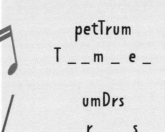

OHIO

STICK THE STATE FLAG HERE →

Ohio has lots of different landscapes to explore: the sandy shores of Lake Erie in the north, the Ohio River snaking along the southern border, and the Appalachian Mountain foothills to the east. It's also a great place for music lovers, who can explore music history at the Rock and Roll Hall of Fame.

FUN FACT

Imagine riding to work through a dark tunnel deep under a lake.

That's what Ohio's salt miners do every day, as they go to work cutting out rock salt from a vast underground cave.

ROCK AND ROLL

Cleveland's Rock and Roll Hall of Fame is a museum that tells the story of rock music, its legendary performers, and its place in our lives. Imagine you're a rock star and doodle yourself here.

Q&A

Ohio is part of the Midwest region. How many other states are in this region? Take a look at the map on pages 4 and 5 if you need a hint.

HEART-SHAPED STATE

Ohio is shaped a bit like a heart. Follow this maze to take a road trip between two of Ohio's biggest cities.

Cleveland

Cincinnati

Nickname: The Buckeye State   State flower: Red carnation   State mammal: White-tailed deer

MICHIGAN

Dense forests, deep lakes, and thousands of miles of shoreline make Michigan a natural wonder. The state mammal, the white-tailed deer, lives in the forest alongside elk and moose. Trees and fish are important natural resources in the state. Michigan's factories make everything from cars to cereal.

STICK THE STATE FLAG HERE

FUN FACT

Michigan is the only state in America that is split into two. The Upper Peninsula to the north connects with the Lower Peninsula down south by the Mackinac Bridge.

GREAT LAKES

The Great Lakes are a group of five massive lakes in North America. They're so big that they contain over 20 percent of Earth's surface freshwater!

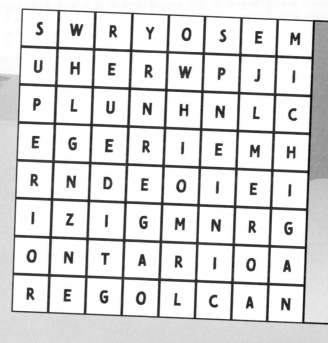

Can you find the names of the five lakes in this word search?

S	W	R	Y	O	S	E	M
U	H	E	R	W	P	J	I
P	L	U	N	H	N	L	C
E	G	E	R	I	E	M	H
R	N	D	E	O	I	E	I
I	Z	I	G	M	N	R	G
O	N	T	A	R	I	O	A
R	E	G	O	L	C	A	N

SUPERIOR
MICHIGAN
HURON
ERIE
ONTARIO

MOTOR CITY

Detroit is the home of Motown music. The word "Motown" comes from Detroit's nickname of Motor City, which it earned because of all the cars made here. Can you place the car stickers in the right order?

INDIANA

The people of Indiana are nicknamed "Hoosiers," although no one is quite sure why. The state's scenery is varied, incuding sand dunes, hills, and rich farmlands. Indiana is known as the crossroads of America because of all its highways, and it's also famous for the Indianapolis 500 race.

FUN FACT
About a quarter of the nation's popcorn comes from Indiana. There's even a town called Popcorn!

33 + 107 + 50

SPEEDY INDIANA

The Indianapolis 500 is one of the most famous car races in the world. The drivers must finish 200 laps of the track to win. Finish these math puzzles to find out who does 200 laps and wins the race.

117 + 82

92 + 98

46 + 146

50 + 25 + 125

STICK THE STATE FLAG HERE

water tower	cornstalk	train
silo	lake	power line
Illinois state license plate	motorcycle	Indiana state license plate

ILLINOIS 999ZZZ

INDIANA 999ZZZ

ROAD TRIP BINGO

More than a dozen interstate highways crisscross Indiana. Challenge someone else to this game of bingo when you're in the car together. Who will be the first to spot three in a row?

Nickname: The Hoosier State   State flower: Peony   State bird: Red cardinal

ILLINOIS

Grassy plains, forests, and rolling hills cover most of Illinois, but it is also home to the nation's third-largest city—Chicago. Illinois is a major transportation hub for ships, trains, and planes, and it's also an important farming state. All kinds of crops grow in its rich soil, from corn and soybeans to pumpkins and apples.

CITY SKYLINE

A huge fire scorched through Chicago in 1871. After the fire, people built the world's first skyscrapers to rise above the city. Design your own skyscraper and doodle it here. Aim high!

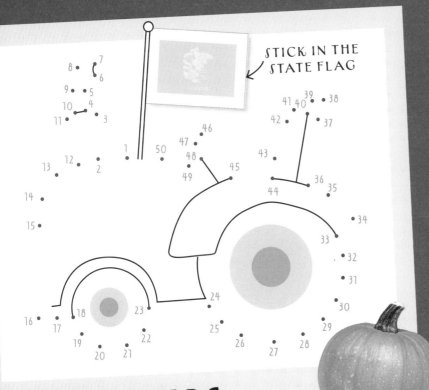

STICK IN THE STATE FLAG

IN THE FIELDS

Around 80 percent of Illinois is farmland. All kinds of crops grow in its rich soil, especially pumpkins. Connect the dots to discover one of the farm vehicles you see all over the state.

FUN FACT

Chicago's nickname, "The Windy City," comes from the the city's chatty politicians, not the breeze blowing off Lake Michigan.

WISCONSIN

This state shares a border with two of the Great Lakes, and has more than 15,000 lakes and 84,000 miles of rivers and streams. Wisconsin is known for its cattle, and the dairy products that are produced here. In fact, people from Wisconsin are called "cheeseheads."

STICK THE STATE FLAG HERE

FUN FACT

Wisconsin has plenty of badgers, but the state nickname—"The Badger State"—comes from state's miners who slept in tunnels.

CHEESY WISCONSIN

Wisconsin is the largest cheesemaking state in the US—about three billion pounds of cheese, of over 300 varieties, are made here each year. Can you unscramble the names of these popular cheeses?

Buel _____   daGou _____

ddChear _____

ellazzarMo _____

wiSss _____   ateF _____

MOO-DOKU

Wisconsin has more dairy cattle than any other state. This sudoku game uses four common dairy products: cheese, ice cream, milk, and yogurt. Fill in the grid with the four symbols, making sure there are no doubles in each row and column.

MINNESOTA

Q&A

Can you name the seven other states that begin with the letter "M." Hint: Check the map on pages 4 and 5.

The Dakota people gave Minnesota its name, which means "sky-blue water." It's the perfect name, since the state has more than 12,000 lakes. The folk hero Paul Bunyan was supposedly born here, and Minnesota raised the first statue to this famous giant.

STICK THE STATE FLAG HERE

BY THE NUMBERS

Minnesota is a big state with a long name. How many numbers can you spell with the letters in its name? Write your answers in the spaces here. (Hint: there are three numbers you can spell.)

_____

_____

_____

FUN FACT

Folktales tell of a giant lumberjack named Paul Bunyan and his blue ox named Babe. It's said that they created Minnesota's lakes with their huge footprints as they traveled the land.

PAUL BUNYAN

Stories say that Paul Bunyan was so big he could chop down an entire forest with one swing of his axe. You can find similar-looking statues of Paul Bunyan all across the US. Can you spot the differences between these two pictures? (Hint: there are 7 differences.)

NORTH DAKOTA

North Dakota is right in the middle of the continent of North America. People have been living here for thousands of years. The state is rich in natural resources, and farms and ranches are spread all over the state. From its vast prairies to the amazing stone formations of the Badlands, North Dakota is a beautiful, wide-open state.

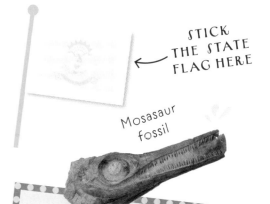

STICK THE STATE FLAG HERE

Mosasaur fossil

FUN FACTS

North Dakota is famous for its waving wheatfields, but in prehistoric times, most of this land was underwater. Many fossils of ancient sea creatures like mosasaurs have been found here.

CROSSING THE GREAT PLAINS

North Dakota is part of the Great Plains, which covers some 2,000 miles from the foothills of the Rocky Mountains to the Mississippi River. Imagine driving a giant combine harvester across these golden grasslands of North Dakota. Place in the stickers and fill in the blanks to find out what wildlife you'd see on your journey.

The yellow-headed

b _ _ c k _ i _ d has a scratchy call that sounds like a rusty gate.

Male bi _ _ _ o r _

s h _ _ _ p have huge horns that can weigh more than all their bones put together.

The spiky y _ c c _ plant has tough leaves and white flowers.

P _ _ a i _ _ e d _ g s live together in underground tunnel "towns."

B _ _ s _ _ n munch their way through weeds and leaves for nearly half the day!

SOUTH DAKOTA

The vast plains of South Dakota are where the buffalo roam, alongside deer and antelope. The grasses in the plains can reach three feet tall, and wildflowers color the land. Its fertile farmland provides lots of crops to the rest of the country, and many fossils have also been dicovered buried in the earth.

STICK THE STATE FLAG HERE

FUN FACTS

Many famous outlaws, lawmen, and frontierswomen from the Wild West era–such as Wyatt Earp and Calamity Jane–lived in Deadwood, South Dakota.

Q&A

Where can you find lots of fossils in South Dakota?

DIGGING UP THE PAST

Mammoth Site near Hot Springs, South Dakota, is famous for its fossils. Can you find all these items at the dig site? Write down the answers using the letter at the top, then the number down the side.

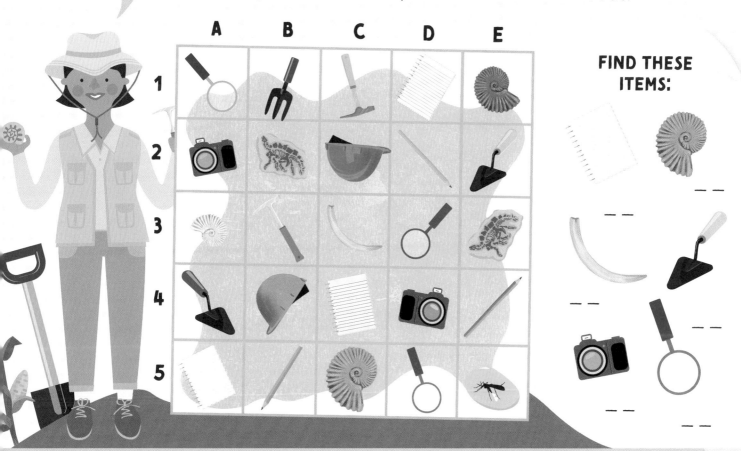

FIND THESE ITEMS:

IOWA

Iowa is famous for its rich soil, left behind when ancient glaciers moved away or melted. Lots of crops are grown here, and it is one of the top producers corn and soybeans. Outside the farms and fields, lots of wild animals roam the countryside.

STICK
THE STATE
FLAG HERE →

FUN FACT

Farming is so important in Iowa that there are more farmyard animals than humans. There are over 20 million pigs and 50 million chickens, but only 3 million people.

WILD ANIMALS

Iowa is home to more than 70 wild mammal species, from huge bison to tiny mice. Can you match the Iowa mammal with its offspring? The first one is done for you.

Q&A

Iowa is a top producer of several different crops. Can you name one of the crops?

Oppossum

Cub

Rabbit

Deer

Fawn

Joey

Beaver

Kitten

Fox

Kit

MISSOURI

Missouri is surrounded by eight other states, so when American settlers began to expand West, many came to start their journey here on the Oregon or Santa Fe Trails. Today, the state is legendary for its jazz and blues music, and a towering monument in the city of St. Louis.

FUN FACT

Missouri has more than 6,000 caves in its state parks. You can take a tour to see the amazing rock formations inside.

↑ STICK THE STATE FLAG HERE

CODE BREAKER

There's an incredible landmark that rises 63 stories into the sky above St. Louis, making it America's tallest man-made monument. Can you crack the code to find the name of this famous St. Louis sight?

CODE: TZGVDZB ZIXS

ANSWER: _ _ _ _ _ _ _   _ _ _ _

CYPHER:
A	B	C	D	E	F	G	H	I	J	K	L	M	N	O
Z	Y	X	W	V	U	T	S	R	Q	P	O	N	M	L

P	Q	R	S	T	U	V	W	X	Y	Z
K	J	I	H	G	F	E	D	C	B	A

HELLO, NEIGHBOR!

Missouri has eight different bordering states, the highest number in the country, along with Tennessee. Can you name all the states? The pictures on each state give you a hint—you can find them on the state pages in this book.

NEBRASKA

The awesome plains of Nebraska stretch as far as the eye can see. More than 400 bird species soar over mammals who live among the grasses. You'll also find amazing rock formations in the Badlands. In the past, many pioneers traveled through these wild lands as they headed west.

FUN FACT

The largest area of sand dunes in the US is nowhere near a beach—it's the Nebraska Sand Hills. They're more than twice the size of Hawaii!

Q&A

Can you name the seven other states that begin with the letter "N." Hint: Check the map on pages 4 and 5.

STICK IN THE STATE FLAG

HEADING WEST

Early pioneers heading west had to cross Nebraska's rough and rocky terrain in covered wagons. Everything a family needed for the long journey was stowed inside. They would also bring cherished possessions to put in their new homes.

Unscramble the words and add the stickers to find some of the items a pioneer family would bring in their wagon.

neMoy

_____

nitFurure

_____

lankBets

_____

retaW

_____

KANSAS

Kansas is famous for its fields of sunflowers out in the plains. It also grows lots of crops like wheat and soybeans. Peanuts are another plant with a connection to Kansas. They're not grown here, but one Kansas native came up with 300 uses for peanuts!

FUN FACT

Amelia Earhart was an amazing pilot from Kansas. She was the first woman to fly solo across the Atlantic.

INCREDIBLE INVENTOR

George Washington Carver was an amazing innovator who lived in Kansas as a teenager. He came up with 300 uses for the peanut, turning it into an important crop for the US.

A	T	M	I	L	K	E	J
D	Y	E	O	S	O	A	P
O	D	D	C	S	L	A	A
Y	I	I	O	D	O	M	P
M	G	C	F	G	T	I	E
B	L	I	F	S	I	R	R
F	U	N	E	S	O	A	R
Z	E	E	E	L	N	A	T

Can you find some of Carver's uses for peanuts in this word search?

**DYE
MEDICINE
SOAP
GLUE
COFFEE
MILK
PAPER
LOTION**

STICK THE STATE FLAG HERE

KANSAS

PUZZLING PAIRS

Just like potatoes, tomatoes, and corn, sunflowers are all American. Back in 3000 BCE, people grew them for oil, food, and dye. In this sunflower patch, not all the blooms are the same. Can you find the pairs that are exactly alike and connect them with a line?

OKLAHOMA

Oklahoma has both natural beauty and exciting cities. Some areas of this state are not really Oklahoma at all–they're governed by Indigenous communities, and are known as sovereign nations.

FUN FACT

The World Championship Cow Chip Throw is held each year in the town of Beaver, Oklahoma. A cow chip is dried cow's poop!

THE FIVE MOONS

"The Five Moons" were five women from Oklahoma. They performed all over the world, and their amazing lives inspired other local Indigenous people from Oklahoma to create art and music about them. Complete this connect-the-dots to find out what the Five Moons were famous for.

STICK THE STATE FLAG HERE

OKLAHOMA

WILD WEATHER

Oklahoma, Texas, New Mexico, and Arizona make up the Southwest region. This region has some extreme weather, with a hot desert climate. Oklahoma also has snow, rain, and tornadoes. Fill in the blank squares using the four weather symbols. Each row and column can only contain one of each symbol.

TEXAS

STICK THE STATE FLAG HERE →

The second-biggest state after Alaska, Texas conjures up images of oil wells and cowboys roaming huge cattle ranches. It is also famous for its space center in Houston, parks, historic buildings, and Tex-Mex cuisine.

FUN FACT

The official sport of Texas is rodeo, in which competitors show off their cowboy skills.

FLAVORSOME FOOD

Texas is famous for its delicious Tex-Mex cuisine. It is influenced by the state's southern neighbor, the country of Mexico. These four friends are at a Tex-Mex restaurant. Figure out how much money each person will have left after paying for their meal.

Sophia has $9 and orders the black bean burrito.

José has $10 and orders the shrimp fajita and cheesy nachos.

Mia has $11 and orders the chicken tacos.

Liam has $10 and orders the beef tamales with dipping sauce.

Black bean burrito $6.75

Shrimp fajita $7

Cheesy nachos $2

Chicken tacos $7.50

Beef tamales with dipping sauce $7.50

THE LONE STAR STATE SONG

Each state has its own song. See if you can crack this code to figure out the first line of the Texas state song. The first three words of the song also happen to be the song's name.

Gvczh, Ifi Gvczh!

_____, ____ _____!

Z Y X W V U T S R Q P O N M L K J I H G F E D C B A
A B C D E F G H I J K L M N O P Q R S T U V W X Y Z

NEW MEXICO

It's no wonder New Mexico's state is nicknamed "The Land of Enchantment." There are ancient ruins made by early Indigenous peoples, and many beautiful natural features, including mountains, forests, canyons, plateaus, and caverns.

STICK IN THE STATE FLAG

FUN FACT

The city of Roswell is famous for an air crash that happened nearby in 1947. Many people still believe that it was a crashed alien spaceship. (In reality, it was just a surveillance balloon!)

COOL CAVES

New Mexico has some truly amazing caves, such as those at Carlsbad Caverns National Park. These huge underground spaces are filled with stalactites (which hang down), stalagmites (which rise up from the cave floor), and columns (when the two meet). Here are two pictures of a cave at Carlsbad Caverns.

CAN YOU SPOT NINE DIFFERENCES BETWEEN THEM?

Nickname: The Land of Enchantment   State flower: Yucca   State mammal: Black bear

ARIZONA

STICK
THE STATE
FLAG HERE

Lots of interesting wildlife can be found in Arizona, many with strange names like "gila monster" and "killdeer." Arizona is known for its deserts and vast forests, but the state's most famous spot is the awesome Grand Canyon, which has its own national park.

FUN FACT
The Grand Canyon, in northern Arizona, is ranked as one of the Seven Natural Wonders of the World.

HELP US GET DOWN THE CANYON.

THE GRAND CANYON

Every year, millions of people come to Grand Canyon National Park to admire the epic views. Complete this maze to help these people ride safely to the bottom of the canyon.

COOL CREATURES

Arizona's animals have some pretty unusual names. Learn about these Arizona animals by placing in the correct sticker for each one.

GILA MONSTER
This lizard is venomous—when it bites, it releases poison.

KILLDEER
This bird's name comes from the sound of its call.

JAVELINA
This piglike animal is also known as a collared peccary.

RINGTAIL
This small mammal was chosen as the state animal in 1986.

COLORADO

Colorado is a state of soaring heights, with the amazing Rocky Mountains rising over the land. The state's towns are the highest in the country, and its beautiful wild landscapes are full of different animals.

STICK THE STATE FLAG HERE

FUN FACT

Colorado is called "The Centennial State" because it became a state exactly 100 years after the signing of the Declaration of Independence.

Q&A
What year did Colorado become a state?

HIDE-AND-SEEK

The American West has plains and several mountain ranges, including the Sierra Nevada and the Rocky Mountains. Can you spot these animals hiding among the Rockies? The first one has been done for you.

 Beaver
B 2

Eagle
_ _

 Black bear
_ _

 Elk
_ _

Coyote
_ _

 Bighorn sheep
_ _

 Snowshoe hare
_ _

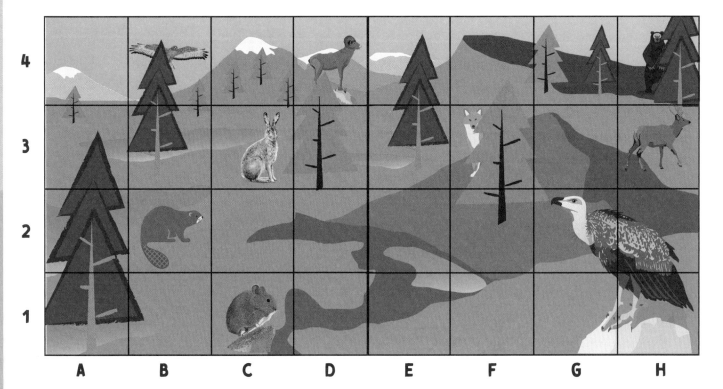

Nickname: The Centennial State   State flower: Rocky Mountain columbine   State mammal: Rocky Mountain bighorn sheep

WYOMING

It may be the tenth largest state, but Wyoming has the fewest people. Its full of wild and wonderful places, and is home to stories of mythical creatures and natural landmarks like the Old Faithful geyser.

FUN FACT

Wyoming's nickname is the Equality State. It got the name because it was the first state to give some women the right to vote, alongside other rights like holding public office.

OLD FAITHFUL

EXPLORING YELLOWSTONE

Yellowstone was America's first national park. It contains half of the world's geysers: boiling hot springs that shoot a column of water into the air. Can you make it from your tent in a Yellowstone campground to see Old Faithful?

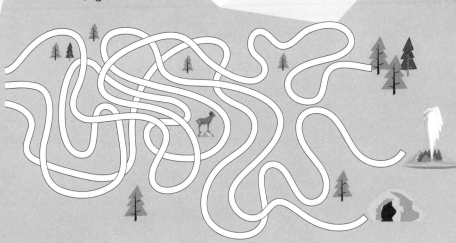

STICK THE STATE FLAG HERE

MYTHICAL CREATURE

The jackalope is a mythical animal with the body of a jackrabbit and the antlers of an antelope. They became a popular myth in Wyoming when a fake jackalope was put on display in a hotel. See if you can draw a jackalope, using these animals as a guide.

MONTANA

Montana is a huge state, covering incredible scenery from glacier-covered mountains to open grasslands. The state is full of wildlife, like bears, as well as valuable resources. Many miners once flocked here to dig up gold, and today Montana produces lots of oil.

FUN FACT

110 different mammal species live in Montana—that's more than any other state! The rarest mammal in the US, the black-footed ferret, is just one animal who lives here.

STICK THE STATE FLAG HERE

THE WILD WEST

The discovery of gold in 1862 led plenty of settlers to Montana. Imagine you could see an old Montana town back in the Gold Rush days. Unscramble these words to learn some of the things you would see.

Tumdleweeb   T _ M B _ _ W E _ D

Coybow   C _ W _ O _

gonWa   _ A G _ N

rifShre   S H _ R _ _ F

noolaS   _ A L _ O N

KNOW YOUR BEARS

There are lots of wild animals in Montana, including both black bears and grizzly bears. They may look similar, but there are some important differences. Here are a list of things to help you spot which bear is which. Take a look at the sign post and draw a line to match each one to the correct bear below.

HUMP ON SHOULDERS

NO SHOULDER HUMP

TALL, POINTY EARS

SHORT, ROUND EARS

SMALLER

BIGGER

GRIZZLY BEAR

BLACK BEAR

Nickname: The Treasure State   State flower: Bitterroot   State mammal: Grizzly bear

IDAHO

Idaho is a beautiful state of mountains and grasslands. It's known as the Gem State because lots of precious stones have found here. But it's also famous for its potatoes—around 13 billion pounds of potatoes are grown here every year.

FUN FACT

Want to feel like you're on the moon without leaving Earth? Travel to Idaho's Craters of the Moon National Monument. Its lunar-like landscape was made by lava from eight volcanic eruptions.

POTATO PUZZLE

In the state capital of Boise, people count down the new year by watching a potato drop, instead of the usual glittery ball. Crack this code to find out some other quirky ways that they celebrate the potato in Idaho.

A	B	C	D	E	F	G	H	I	J	K	L	M
1	2	3	4	5	6	7	8	9	10	11	12	13

N	O	P	Q	R	S	T	U	V	W	X	Y	Z
14	15	16	17	18	19	20	21	22	23	24	25	26

Q&A

What's the name of the Idaho national monument that looks just like the moon?

You can spend the night in a room shaped like a potato

8	15	20	5	12

_____

Come here to learn all about potatoes

13	21	19	5	21	13

_____

Ice cream made to look like a potato

19	21	14	4	1	5

_____

A big event held in Shelley

19	16	21	4		4	1	25

_____

SPARKLY SCRAMBLE

Almost every type of gem has been found in Idaho, including one of the largest diamonds ever found in the US. Can you unscramble the names of these sparkly Idaho treasures?

Diadnom _____

edaJ _____

perJas _____

zopaT _____

lOpa _____

STICK THE STATE FLAG HERE

UTAH

With five national parks, Utah has some of the most incredible scenery in the United States. Many dinosaur fossils have been discovered in these ancient, rocky landscapes. Utah was also an important stop for pioneers traveling west in the 19th century.

Q&A
What is a hoodoo?

FUN FACT
You can spot some incredible rock shapes in Utah, from strange spires to hoodoos: weird towers with a hat of hard rock.

RIDING THE RAILS

A coast-to-coast railroad opened in 1869, making it easier to cross the vast United States. The last spike was hammered into the tracks at Promontory Summit, Utah. Can you help these trains meet at Promontory Summit?

STICK THE STATE FLAG HERE

PROMONTORY SUMMIT

← Apatosaurus

↑ Allosaurus

Stegosaurus

Dryosaurus

DINO SUDOKU

Today, dino fossils are found all over Utah. You can see their big bones buried in the rocks at Dinosaur National Monument. Fill in this grid with these four Utah dinosaurs. Each row and column can only contain one of each dino—no doubles!

Q&A
What is the name for ancient drawings and patterns carved into rock?

NEVADA

With snowy mountains, dry deserts, and America's largest alpine lake, Nevada is packed with natural beauty. It's also full of history, exciting cities, and amazing landmarks, making Nevada an incredible place to travel and explore.

TRAVEL NEVADA

Here are five great places to visit in Nevada. Draw lines to connect the matching set of descriptions, photos, and fun facts.

KEY FACTS

STICK THE STATE FLAG HERE

WHAT'S IN NEVADA?

THEMED HOTELS

BEAUTIFUL NATURAL SCENERY

ANCIENT ROCK ART

WILD WEST HISTORY

IMPRESSIVE ENGINEERING

Lake Tahoe

Las Vegas

Virginia City

Hoover Dam

Sloan Canyon Petroglyph Site

Provides electricity for 1.3 million people in three different states.

Petroglyphs are rock art made by early Indigenous peoples.

The most expensive hotel room in this city costs $100,000 a night.

You can hang out at the beach in summer, or ski here in winter.

Lots of miners moved here to get rich from silver.

FUN FACT
Nevada may be called the Silver State, but it is the leading producer of gold in the US.

CALIFORNIA

California has a bit of everything. There are forests and mountains in the north, deserts to the south, and beautiful beaches up and down the West Coast. California is famous for its exciting cities, its amazing landmarks, and its incredible wildlife.

STICK THE STATE FLAG HERE

CALIFORNIA'S WILDLIFE

California has very diverse wildlife because of all the different environments. Can you fill in the name of each animal?

The California

co _ d _ r

is a very rare bird.

The state land mammal is the California

g _ _ z _ l y
b _ a _ .

S _ a
l _ o _ s

sunbathe on piers and rocks.

P _ p f _ s _

are fish that live in the desert of Death Valley.

Q&A
Name three places in California. Hint: you can find lots of examples on this page.

S e _
_ t t _ _ s

can float on their backs.

54

SAY HELLO!

Here are the most common languages spoken in California. Unscramble the words to work out which language each "hello" is written in.

FUN FACT

California's redwoods are the tallest trees in the world! Two places you can see them are Muir Woods National Monument and Redwood National and State Park.

KAMUSTA

logTaga

T _ g _ l _ g

HOLA

anSpish

_ p a _ i s _

NI HAO

Chesein

C h _ _ e _ _

HELLO

ishgIEn

_ n g _ _ _ h

XIN CHAO

neseVietam

V i _ t n a _ e _ _

STATE SIGHTS

Here are some of California's most famous places. Fill in the stickers, then look for the words in the grid.

A	W	R	Y	O	S	E	M	I	T	E
W	Z	S	A	C	D	J	E	Y	I	L
O	L	A	N	I	N	L	U	M	P	T
Y	G	N	I	D	R	M	F	O	R	Y
M	N	D	E	G	S	I	R	N	A	I
B	B	I	G	S	U	R	A	T	S	H
F	R	E	R	S	O	S	R	E	Q	I
Z	E	G	A	L	C	A	T	R	A	Z
A	Y	O	O	T	Z	U	O	E	W	A
T	E	K	D	I	A	T	S	Y	I	E
H	O	L	L	Y	W	O	O	D	T	L

Hollywood

Yosemite

Monterey

Alcatraz

San Diego

Big Sur

TOP OF
HELLS
CANYON

OREGON

Oregon's state's forests are home to wildlife such as wolves, elk, and owls. The sleek beavers who give Oregon its nickname glide through the state's rivers. Oregon is also full of natural wonders, from the soaring peak of Mt. Hood to Crater Lake, the deepest lake in the US. You'll find the deepest river gorge on the western Oregon border, too.

FUN FACT

Bigfoot is a legendary creature said to roam the Oregon wilderness. Oregon has the world's only Bigfoot trap in the Siskiyou National Forest. It has never been filled.

BOTTOM
OF HELLS
CANYON

STATE FLAG

Oregon is the only state in the US with a two-sided flag. You can see the front of the flag below. What design would you put on the back? (To find out what's really on the back of Oregon's flag, take a look at the state animal listed on this page.)

HELLS CANYON

Oregon's Hells Canyon is the deepest gorge in North America, at 7,993 ft deep. How many Empire State Buildings could you stack up in the giant gorge? Use your finger and thumb to measure the skyscraper on the left. Then see how many times it would fit into the picture of the canyon on this page.

EMPIRE
STATE
BUILDING

STICK THE
STATE FLAG
HERE

STATE OF OREGON
1859

Nickname: The Beaver State   State flower: Oregon grape   State mammal: American beaver

WASHINGTON

Volcanoes helped to shape this land, and old lava fields spread across the state. Half of Washington is covered in forests, but its also got plenty of exciting cities. The biggest city, Seattle, is especially famous for its Space Needle and thriving tech companies.

← SPACE NEEDLE

TECH EVOLUTION

Washington is a world leader in innovation and technology. You may know all about the gadgets of today, but what about where it all began? Try to sort these devices into pairs—one is the old version, and one is the familiar modern style. There are some clues to help you figure out the older gadgets.

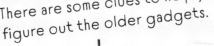

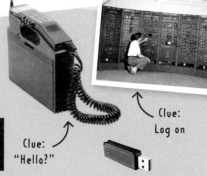

Clue: Extra memory

Clue: "Hello?"

Clue: Log on

STICK IN THE STATE FLAG

FUN FACT

Washington's Boeing Everett Factory includes the world's largest building by volume (inside space). It has to be big because airplanes are built here. Staff use tricycles to get around!

Q&A

What's the name of the biggest city in Washington?

MARMOT MAZE

The state land mammal is a cat-sized rodent with a bushy tail, called the Olympic marmot. These furry animals are found nowhere else in the world. They are chatty and active, but come fall they hibernate. Can you help this marmot find its den?

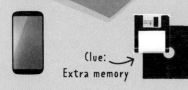

HAWAII

HAWAIIAN ISLANDS

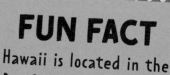

STICK THE STATE FLAG HERE

The most recent state to join the Union, Hawaii lies in the Pacific Ocean, about 2,000 miles from the mainland United States. Its islands boast beautiful beaches, tropical forests, and a wealth of wildlife both on land and in the Pacific Ocean.

FUN FACT

Hawaii is located in the Pacific Ocean, far from the mainland United States. It is the only US state that is made up entirely of islands.

ALOHA!

SCUBA FUN

The ocean surrounding the Hawaiian islands is a treasure trove of awesome creatures. Scuba divers travel from all over the world to swim with marine widlife here. Find the stickers that complete the scene, and unscramble the names of the animals.

knMo leaS

_____

This creature is Hawaii's state animal.

pholDin

_____

This sea mammal is known for being very intelligent.

Q&A

Which type of fish lives with a sea anemone?

gnaT

_____

This fish has sharp spines near its tail.

eaS rtTule

_____

Only the females of this reptile ever return to land, so they can lay eggs.

HAWAIIAN LANGUAGE

Hawaii is the only US state with two official languages—English and Hawaiian. Here are some Hawaiian words you may have heard. See if you can find them in the word search.

X	A	L	O	H	A	N	H
J	N	F	C	E	I	V	U
B	U	H	P	A	K	L	L
C	H	N	L	E	I	N	A
U	A	U	L	M	W	I	K
D	K	D	C	N	E	N	E
N	E	L	E	L	U	K	U
O	P	S	O	T	N	R	B

↑ YELLOW HIBISCUS

ALOHA
Hello or goodbye

HULA
Type of dance

UKULELE
Small instrument

WIKI
Fast

LUAU
Traditional feast

LEI
Garland of flowers

KAHUNA
Important or wise person

NENE
Hawaiian goose

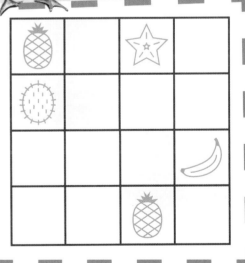

HINT: some words may run backward or upward.

FRUIT FUN

Many types of delicious fruits are grown in Hawaii. Fill in the blank squares using these four fruits. Each row and column can only contain one of each fruit.

PINEAPPLE

RAMBUTAN

 STARFRUIT

BANANA

lownC shiF

This fish lives among the tentacles of a sea anemone.

aSe Amonene

This animal is related to jellyfish.

ALASKA

A vast wilderness northwest of Canada, Alaska is the largest state—more than twice the size of second-largest, Texas. Despite its size, it has the third-smallest populaton. While it does have cool cities, Alaska is mostly famous for its beautiful natural landscapes and magnificent animals.

WONDERFUL WILDLIFE

Alaska is home to a wealth of wildlife. You can see marine life such as whales along the coast. Farther inland, the forests and mountains are home to bears, caribou, musk oxen, moose, and all kinds of birds. Can you spot nine differences between these two river scenes?

Q&A
Can you name three large mammals that live in Alaska?

EXPLORING ALASKA

There are lots of different ways to explore the Alaskan landscapes. Draw a line to link match each vehicle with the correct journey.

Making a long journey between the cities of Juneau and Anchorage

Riding to Fairbanks to see the northern lights

Cycling in Denali National Park

Exploring the rivers

Cruising near the coast to see glaciers

STICK THE STATE FLAG HERE

FUN FACT

Denali is the highest mountain in North America. Walter Harper became the first person to climb to the summit, in 1913.

ALASKAN SNACKS

When you're visiting a new place, it's fun to try new foods and snacks. You may even find a new favorite dish! If you had $15 to spend, which of these Alaskan foods would you try?

How much money would you have left?

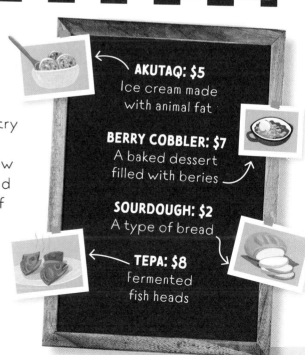

AKUTAQ: $5
Ice cream made with animal fat

BERRY COBBLER: $7
A baked dessert filled with beries

SOURDOUGH: $2
A type of bread

TEPA: $8
Fermented fish heads

ANSWERS

P.7 ACROSS THE 50 STATES
GREAT STATE SOUVENIRS:
Statue of Liberty - New York
Maple Syrup - Vermont
Sea Otter Cuddly Toy - California
Toy Rocket - Florida
Popcorn Keyring - Indiana
Cowboy Hat - Texas

COUNTRY COLLAGE:

P.8 MAINE
OH, BUOY!:

VIKINGS Maine, penny, America, Europe.

P.9 NEW HAMPSHIRE
FALL LEAVES:

COUNT UP: 7 people are taking photos. There are 4 dogs.

P.10 VERMONT
STATE SYMBOLS:

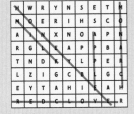

P.11 MASSACHUSETTS
MAYFLOWER MAZE:

FAMOUS SIGHTS Cape Cod, Freedom Trail, Harvard University.

P.12 RHODE ISLAND
13 COLONIES: 1: Georgia, 2: Pennsylvania, 3: New York, 4: New Jersey, 5: New Hampshire, 6: Massachusetts, 7: North Carolina, 8: Connecticut, 9: Delaware, 10: South Carolina, 11: Rhode Island, 12: Maryland, 13: Virginia.

P.13 CONNECTICUT
Q&A: True.
ANIMAL TRACKS:

P.14-15 NEW YORK
Q&A: False.
GREAT OUTDOORS:

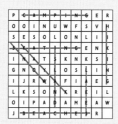

NEW YORK NEW YORK: There are 6 flags.

THOUSAND ISLANDS: 1,864.

P.16 PENNSYLVANIA
Q&A: The Liberty Bell.
SPRING FORECAST: Groundhog.

FOOD-OKU:

P.17 NEW JERSEY
Q&A: Three states: Delaware, Pennsylvania, and New York.

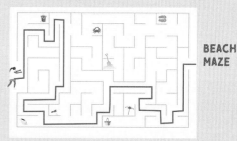

BEACH MAZE

FOREST TREES: Hickory, Maple, Oak, Beech, Pine.

P.18 DELAWARE
MAP IT: Rhode Island [6], Delaware [5], North Dakota [4], South Dakota [3], Texas [2], Alaska [1]

P.19 MARYLAND
MARINE LIFE:

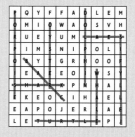

P.20 WEST VIRGINIA
Q&A: It's the only state that is completely inside the Appalachian Mountains.

WILD WEST VIRGINIA: flying squirrel, black bear, rabbit, duck, turkey, deer.

P.21 VIRGINIA
HISTORIC VIRGINIA:

WASHINGTON, DC: Washington Monument, Lincoln Memorial, The White House.

P.22 KENTUCKY
Q&A: 7

CORN MAZE:

P.23 TENNESSEE

MUSIC FESTIVAL:

HOW MANY: Guitars: 4, Ice creams: 6, Saxophones: 3.

P.25 SOUTH CAROLINA

DINNERTIME:

DAY AT THE BEACH: Ava - $2.50, Elijah - $1.75, William - $3.25

P.26 GEORGIA

GEORGIA FACTS: Atlanta, Airport, Treasure, Aquarium, Peaches, Mountains.

FLY AWAY:

P.27 FLORIDA

Q&A: True.

BLAST OFF: Saturn V.

GATORS AND CROCS:
Alligator – Round snout, Usually darker in color, Has a shorter body.
Crocodile – Long, pointy snout, Usually lighter in color, Has a longer body.

P.28 ALABAMA

Q&A: 1978.

STATE SUDOKU:

P.29 MISSISSIPPI

BEAST OF THE BAYOU:

MISSISSIPPI MUD PIE MATH:
One-half or ½, Three-fourths or ¾, Two-thirds or ⅔.

P.30 ARKANSAS

URBAN ARKANSAS:

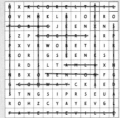

P.31 LOUISIANA

DELICIOUS DESERTS:

ALL THAT JAZZ:
Trumpet, Drums, Piano, Saxophone Clarinet, Trombone.

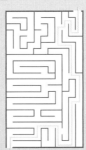

P.32 OHIO

Q&A: 12.

HEART SHAPED STATE:

P.33 MICHIGAN

GREAT LAKES:

MOTOR CITY:

P.34 INDIANA

SPEEDY INDIANA: Red = 1st (200), Blue = 2nd (199), Green = 3rd (192), Yellow/Purple = 4th (190)

P.36 WISCONSIN

CHEESY WISCONSIN: Blue, Gouda, Cheddar, Mozzarella, Swiss, Feta.

MOO-DOKU:

P.37 MINNESOTA

Q&A: Maine, Maryland, Massachusetts, Michigan, Mississippi, Missouri, Montana.

BY THE NUMBERS: One, Nine, Ten.

PAUL BUNYAN:

P.38 NORTH DAKOTA

CROSSING THE GREAT PLAINS:
Blackbird, Yucca, Bison, Prairie dogs, Bighorn sheep.

P.39 SOUTH DAKOTA

Q&A: Mammoth Site.

DIGGING UP THE PAST:

A5   C5   C3   E2   A2   D5

P.40 IOWA

Q&A: Corn or Soybeans.

BABY MATCH-UP: Opossum + joey, Beaver + kit, Fox + cub, Rabbit + kitten, Deer + fawn.

P.41 MISSOURI

HELLO, NEIGHBOR!: Iowa, Illinois, Kentucky, Tennessee, Arkansas, Oklahoma, Kansas, Nebraska.

CODEBREAKER: Gateway Arch.

P.42 NEBRASKA

Q&A: Nevada, New Hampshire, New Jersey, New Mexico, New York, North Carolina, North Dakota.

HEADING WEST: money, furniture, blankets, water.

P.43 KANSAS

INCREDIBLE INVENTOR:

A	T	M	I	L	K	E	J
D	Y	O	S	O	A	A	P
O	D	D	C	S	L	A	A
Y	I	I	O	D	O	M	P
M	G	C	F	G	T	I	E
B	L	I	F	S	I	R	R
F	U	N	E	S	O	A	R
Z	E	E	E	L	N	A	T

PUZZLING PAIRS:

P.44 OKLAHOMA

WILD WEATHER:

P.45 TEXAS

FLAVORSOME FOOD: Sophia: $2.25, José: £1, Mia: $3.50, Liam: $2.50.

THE LONE STAR STATE SONG: Texas, our Texas!

P.46 NEW MEXICO

COOL CAVES:

P.46 ARIZONA

GRAND CANYON:

P.48 COLORADO

Q&A: 1876.   **HIDE AND SEEK:**

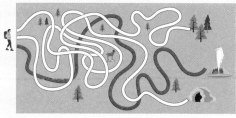

B4   H4   H3   F3   D4   C3

P.49 WYOMING

EXPLORING YELLOWSTONE:

P.48 MONTANA

THE WILD WEST: Tumbleweed, Cowboy, Wagon, Sheriff, Saloon.

KNOW YOUR BEARS: Grizzly bear – Hump on shoulder, Short, round ears, Bigger. Black bear – No shoulder hump, Tall, pointy ears, Smaller.

P.51 IDAHO

Q&A: Craters of the Moon National Monument.

POTATO PUZZLE: Hotel, Museum, Sundae, Spud Day.

SPARKLY SCRAMBLE: Diamond, Jade, Jasper, Topaz, Opal.

P.52 UTAH

Q&A: Naturally formed rock towers with what looks like a rock hat on top.

RIDING THE RAILS:

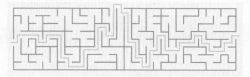

DINO SUDOKU:

P.53 NEVADA

Q&A: Petroglyphs.

TRAVEL NEVADA: Themed hotels / Las Vegas / The most expensive hotel room in this city costs $100,000 a night.
Beautiful natural scenery / Lake Tahoe / You can hang out at the beach in summer, or ski here in winter.
Ancient rock art / Sloan Canyon Petroglyph Site / Petroglyphs are rock art made by early Indigenous peoples.
Wild West history / Virginia City / Lots of miners moved here to get rich from silver.
Impressive engineering / Hoover Dam / Provides electricity for 1.3 million people in three different states.

P.54-55 CALIFORNIA

Q&A: Sacramento, Death Valley, Hollywood, Yosemite, Monterey, Alcatraz, San Diego, Big Sur, Muir Woods National Monument, Redwood National and State Park.

CALIFORNIA'S WILDLIFE: Sea lions, grizzly bear, condor, Pupfish, Sea otters.

SAY HELLO!: Tagalog, Spanish, Chinese, English, Vietnamese.

STATE SIGHTS:

A	W	R	Y	O	S	E	M	I	T	E
W	Z	S	A	C	D	J	E	Y	I	L
O	L	N	N	I	N	L	U	P	P	T
Y	G	N	I	D	R	M	F	O	R	Y
M	N	S	E	G	S	I	R	A	A	I
B	B	I	G	S	U	R	A	T	S	H
F	R	E	R	S	O	S	R	E	Q	I
Z	E	S	A	L	C	A	T	A	Z	Z
A	Y	Q	O	T	Z	U	O	E	W	A
T	E	K	D	I	A	T	S	I	E	
H	O	L	L	Y	W	O	O	D	T	L

P.56 OREGON

HELL'S CANYON: 5, with a little room left over.

P.57 WASHINGTON

Q&A: Seattle.
TECH EVOLUTION:

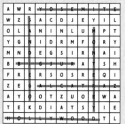

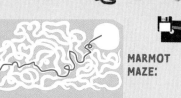

MARMOT MAZE:

P.58 HAWAII

Q&A: clown fish.

SCUBA FUN: Monk Seal, Tang, Dolphin, Sea Turtle, Clown Fish, Sea Anemone.

HAWAIIAN LANGUAGE:

X	A	L	O	H	A	N	H
J	N	F	C	E	I	V	U
B	U	H	P	A	K	L	L
C	H	N	L	E	N	A	
U	A	U	L	M	W	I	K
D	K	D	C	N	E	N	E
N	E	L	E	L	U	K	U
O	P	S	O	T	N	R	S

FRUIT FUN:

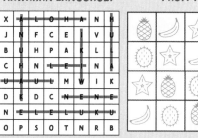

P.60-61 ALASKA

Q&A: brown bear, black bear, moose, caribou, mountain goat, wolf.

WONDERFUL WILDLIFE:

EXPLORING ALASKA: Making a long journey between the cities of Juneau and Anchorage (Airplane)
Riding to Fairbanks to see the northern lights (Train)
Cycling in Denali National Park (Bicycle)
Exploring the rivers (Kayak)
Cruising near the coast to see glaciers (Ship)

64

FLAGS

Add each state flag sticker to the correct page. The USA flag goes on page 3.

USA

Alabama

Alaska

Arizona

Arkansas

California

Colorado

Connecticut

Delaware

Florida

Georgia

Hawaii

Idaho

Illinois

Indiana

Iowa

Kansas

Kentucky

Louisiana

Maine

Maryland

Massachusetts

Michigan

Minnesota

Mississippi

Missouri

Montana

Nebraska

Nevada

New Hampshire

New Jersey

New Mexico

New York

North Carolina

North Dakota

Ohio

Oklahoma

Oregon

Pennsylvania

Rhode Island

South Carolina

South Dakota

Tennessee

Texas

Utah

Vermont

Virginia

Washington

West Viginia

Wisconsin

Wyoming

PAGE 4
The 50 States

PAGE 11
Massachussets

Harvard University →

Cape Cod

Freedom Trail

PAGE 18 Delaware

3rd

5th

2nd

1st

4th

PAGE 20 West Virginia

Rabbit

Turkey

Black Bear

Flying Squirrel

Deer

Ducks

PAGE 29
Mississippi

Ant   Muskrat   Crab   Catfish

PAGE 33 Michigan

PAGE 38 North Dakota

Blackbird

Bison

Prairie Dog

Yucca

Bighorn Sheep

PAGE 40

North Dakota

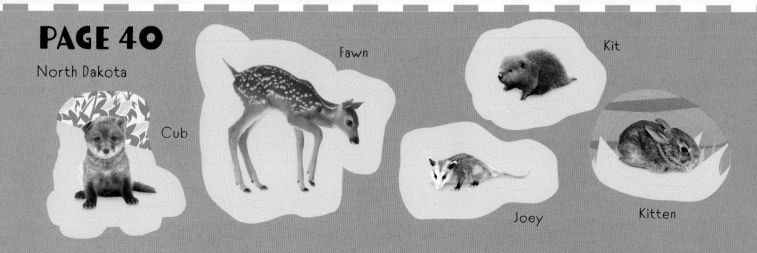

Fawn

Kit

Cub

Joey

Kitten

PAGE 42-43

Mississippi

Money   Water   Blankets   Furniture

PAGE 47

Arizona

Gila monster   Killdeer   Javelina   Ringtail

PAGE 55 California

Big Sur   Yosemite   Alcatraz   Hollywood   San Diego   Monterey

PAGE 58-59

Hawaii

Tang

Dolphin

Sea Turtle

Clown Fish